All About
JAPAN
Stories, Songs, Crafts
and Games for Kids

WILLAMARIE MOORE

Illustrated by

KAZUMI WILDS

TUTTLE Publishing

Tokyo | Rutland, Vermont | Singapore

Contents

Konnichi-wa!
こんにちは

That means **"Hello!"** My name is Yuto. I am 10 years old, and I'm the oldest of the kids in my family. My younger sister is 6 years old, and she just started going to elementary school. We have a baby brother who was born last year.

At school, I'm in the 5th grade. Because we live in the country, our school is small—there are only 12 kids in my grade. And we have all been in school together ever since kindergarten, so we all know each other really well. *(More about my school on page 27!)*

School is okay. My favorite class is art, because I like drawing. I also like collecting bugs, especially the giant samurai beetles. I like drawing the different kinds of bugs I've found. I have created my own **manga** (comic strip) character, a samurai beetle who saves the world from destruction. *(More about manga on page 55!)*

Hajimemashite!
はじめまして

That means **"Nice to meet you!"** My name is Momoka. I live
with my parents in Tokyo, but we travel a lot, too. *(Check out my favorite places, on
page 13!)* This year I turned 12 years old. My grandma calls me a "very active
girl." My favorite sport is skiing, which my whole family does in the winter, and
in the summer, I love to swim.

I also take ballet lessons, **shodo** (calligraphy) lessons, and this year I've started going
to **juku** (cram school) after school, to prepare for the entrance exams for junior high
school. I guess my grandma is right: I have quite a busy life! *(Learn more about a typical
day in my life on page 24!)*

I'm an only child. We live in a condo in a tall building in Tokyo. *(Check out my bedroom
on page 18!)* My dad is a "salaryman." He works for a big advertising company. My mom is
a professor at Sophia University. *(More about my family on page 25!)*

Your Map of Japan

Japan is an island country. There are more than 3,000 islands stretching for 3,000 kilometers (1,864 miles) from north to south. The four main islands are **Hokkaido**, **Honshu**, **Shikoku**, and **Kyushu**. The total area of the country is about the same as the country of Germany, or the U.S. state of California.

Japan is located in the part of the world called the "Ring of Fire," so there are many hot springs, earthquakes, and volcanoes. 80% of the land is covered by mountains. **Mt. Fuji** is Japan's tallest mountain. It is 3,776 meters (12,388 feet) tall.

← Japan

"We learn in school that Japan is shaped like a seahorse. Can you see that by looking at this map?"

KORE

6

3

1

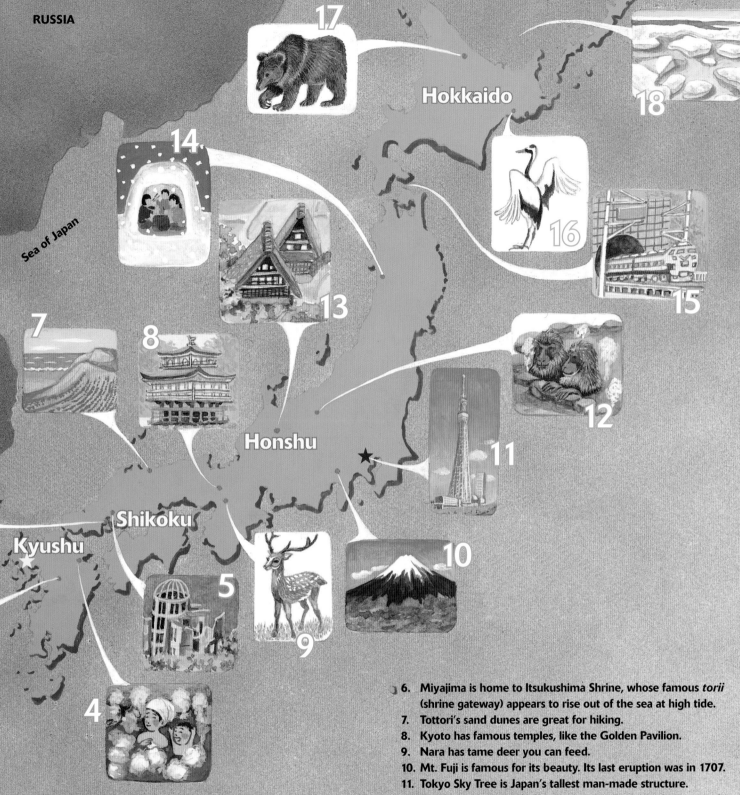

RUSSIA

Hokkaido

Sea of Japan

Honshu

Shikoku

Kyushu

Can you find these locations?

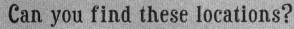

⭐ Yuto lives here!   ★ Momoka lives here!

1. Okinawa is where Iriomote wildcats live.
2. Tropical fruits grow in Japan!
3. Mt. Aso is the largest active volcano in Japan.
4. Beppu is famous for its many hot springs.
5. The A-Bomb Dome in Hiroshima was the only building left standing in the area where the first atomic bomb exploded on August 6, 1945.

6. Miyajima is home to Itsukushima Shrine, whose famous *torii* (shrine gateway) appears to rise out of the sea at high tide.
7. Tottori's sand dunes are great for hiking.
8. Kyoto has famous temples, like the Golden Pavilion.
9. Nara has tame deer you can feed.
10. Mt. Fuji is famous for its beauty. Its last eruption was in 1707.
11. Tokyo Sky Tree is Japan's tallest man-made structure.
12. The famous snow monkeys love to bathe in the hot springs!
13. Historic *gassho*-style thatched-roof farmhouses helped protect villagers from the heavy snow in this region.
14. The city of Yokote is famous for the annual Kamakura Matsuri, the Japanese Igloo Festival!
15. The Seikan Tunnel, the longest underwater tunnel in the world, connects Honshu and Hokkaido.
16. In folklore, the crane is said to live for 1,000 years, so in Japan it's a symbol for long life.
17. You don't want to mess with the Hokkaido Brown Bear!
18. *Ryuhyo* (drift ice) in the Sea of Okhotsk attracts tourists.

Springtime Cherry Blossoms

Spring is the time for new beginnings. In April, the new school year starts for children. Companies start the new business year. And throughout most of Japan, the cherry blossoms bloom!

Sakura is the Japanese word for "cherry blossom." When the sakura are in full bloom, people make special visits to parks and other spots with many cherry trees. They enjoy picnicking under the beautiful blossoms, and sometimes sing their favorite songs with a portable karaoke machine!

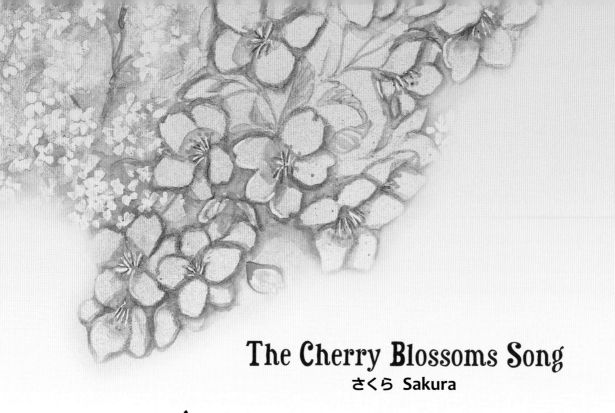

The Cherry Blossoms Song
さくら Sakura

さくら　さくら　やよいの　そらは
Sa - ku - ra sa - ku - ra ya - yo - i no so - ra wa
Cherry blossoms, cherry blossoms, across the spring sky,

みわたす　かぎり　かすみか　くもか
Mi - wa - ta - su ka - gi - ri ka - su - mi ka ku - mo ka
As far as you can see. Is it a mist, or clouds?

においぞ　いずる　いざや　いざや
Ni - o - i zo i - zu - ru i - za - ya i - za - ya
Fragrant in the air. Come now, come,

み　に　ゆ　か　ん
mi ni yu - ka - n
Let's look, at last!

This is one of the most well known traditional Japanese songs. It is often played on a **koto**, a traditional Japanese stringed instrument.

Writing Haiku Poems

Another favorite Japanese pastime is to make up poetry for the season. A **haiku** is a 17-syllable poem that references the season. There are a few basic rules for writing a proper **haiku**:

- The first line has **5 syllables**.

- The second line has **7 syllables**.

- The third line has **5 syllables**.

- You must include a **kigo**, or "seasonal word," to symbolize which season you are writing about. For example: cherry blossoms indicate spring, cicadas mean summer, maple leaves mean fall, snow means winter.

What season is it now, where you are? Can you create a **haiku** to express your feelings about it? Here is an example to inspire you, by the Japanese poet Issa . . .

雪とけて
Yuki tokete
After the snows melt

村いっぱいの
Mura ippai no
Village once filled with white drifts

子ども哉
Kodomo ka na
Full again with kids

—Issa

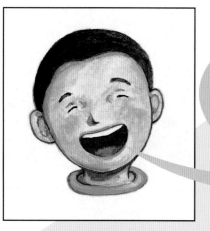

"My three favorite places in Japan are..."

Nara is famous for the deer that wander around in the large park area where many historic buildings are. On your way to visit the temples, you can **pet the deer** and feed them special rice crackers.

The largest Buddha statue in the world is inside the Great Buddha Hall of Todai-ji Temple. The Buddha is 15 meters (49.2 feet) tall and it weighs about 300 tons! One fun thing for kids is to crawl through a hole at the base of a pillar behind the statue. They say the hole is exactly the same size as the Great Buddha's nostril, and that if you crawl through it, you will be healthy and happy in life.

Nebuta Matsuri is a huge, weeklong street festival and parade in Aomori. Everyone can participate! ...That is, as long as you wear the proper costume, called **haneto**.

There's a special hat, a special waistband with a canteen hanging from it, and special shoes. The festival's main attraction is the nighttime parade of floats that are actually gigantic paper lanterns shaped like famous samurai warriors. They are made of bamboo or wood frames covered with paper. They are lit from inside with hundreds of light bulbs. It's an amazing sight to see!

Hiroshima Peace Memorial Park has so many different monuments. There is the A-bomb Dome, which I had seen pictures of, but is huge and scary to see with your own eyes. Then there is the Children's Peace Monument, which displays **thousands of origami cranes**, sent from children all over the world!

At the Peace Memorial Museum, they display all kinds of items that were frozen in time, at exactly 8:15 AM on August 6, 1945, the moment when the bomb was dropped. It's kind of spooky, and makes you realize how awful war is. I wish for no more nuclear weapons and guns on earth! I want peace in the world.

"These are my three favorite places..."

Sapporo Snow Festival or Yuki Matsuri is held in the

wintertime on Hokkaido, the northernmost of Japan's main islands. (The word **yuki** means snow—like in that **haiku** on page 11!—and **matsuri** means festival, a word you'll see more of later in this book.)

In Odori Koen, the central park in the middle of the city, people make huge sculptures (there's about 300 of them) out of ice and snow. They really are HUGE...some as big as buildings and you can walk through them!

Okinawa is the southernmost string of islands in

Japan, and the only prefecture that is located in the **subtropical** climate zone.

What is most surprising is how blue the ocean water is! And the sand is so white that it hurts your eyes! And then once you go into the water, it is so clear, you can see right to the bottom. You can also visit the Ocean Expo Park, and check out the most amazing whale sharks and manta rays!

The Island-Hopping Road or Shimanami Kaido is a fun adventure

to bicycle along. It's a route that's 80 km (50 miles) long and it **connects six islands** between Honshu and Shikoku.

And there's a special route only for bicycle and foot traffic. Don't forget to pack **onigiri** for lunch—the perfect picnic or travel-food! *(Check out page 23 to learn how to make onigiri!)*

The Myth of Japan's Creation

Izanagi and Izanami Create the Universe

In the beginning, the world was formless and shapeless, just a sea of filmy fog. Then a reed began growing high, and from it were born eight generations of gods.

One day, the first gods chose two divine beings—Izanagi (who was male) and Izanami (who was female)—to create the first land. The gods gave them a jeweled staff and showed them the Bridge of Heaven, which floated between Heaven and Earth.

At first, Izanagi and Izanami did not know what to do. They stood on the Bridge and looked down at the churning liquid below. They dipped the staff in and stirred it around. When they pulled it out, a few drops fell and became solid: this was the first island. Izanagi and Izanami were so pleased with this result, they descended from the Bridge and onto the new island.

They found it so pleasant, they decided to stay there. They built a home and had many, many children, some of whom later became the Islands of Japan.

One of their children was Amaterasu, the Sun Goddess. Her grandson, Ninigi, was sent to rule Japan. He was given three treasures as symbols of his rule: a jeweled necklace (to symbolize generosity and kindness), a mirror (meaning purity), and a sword (courage).

It is said that Ninigi's great-grandson, Jimmu Tenno, became the first human Emperor of Japan. Since him, there have been 125 Emperors of Japan—the longest unbroken line of emperors in the world. A necklace, mirror and sword are still the Japanese imperial symbols today.

Royal Symbols

The green jade bead is a *magatama*, a curved bead from ancient times. It is what the imperial necklace is said to be made of. The sword and the round mirror are also ancient treasures.

The Age of Nobility

Around the 7th century, people began building cities. The first capital was Nara, and then in the year 794, Kyoto became the capital. The nobility became more powerful. The Japanese writing called *kana* was invented, and the world's first novel, *The Tale of Genji*, was written by Lady Murasaki.

The Age of Warriors

Samurai warriors became more powerful. They were loyal to a *daimyo* (feudal lord). The different lords' armies battled each other throughout the country. Great castles were built for defense but also to display wealth and power.

Pre-History

Around 2500 BCE, people used stone tools and earthenware. Around 1760 BCE they began to use metal tools and grow rice. Around 300–400 CE, they built burial mounds with *haniwa* figures like this, made of clay.

The Age of Opening to the World

With the arrival of U.S. Commodore Perry's Black Ships in 1853, Japan agreed to trade with other countries. In 1868, the Meiji Restoration put the Emperor back in power, in Kyoto. The capital city of Edo was given a new name, Tokyo, and this is where political rule remained. Many big changes took place in the way people lived.

The Age of Merchants

Under one ruler again, more people lived in cities. As they bought and sold more and more goods, merchants became more powerful. New art forms like *kabuki* and *ukiyo-e* became very popular, especially among townspeople.

Japan Today

Japan is a major economic and cultural power in the world.

A Walk Through Japanese History

"Welcome to my home!"

Our apartment is called a "2LDK." This means we have two bedrooms, a living/dining room, and a kitchen. Even though our apartment is small, I have my own room, which is better than a lot of kids. I like decorating it exactly the way I want.

We live in the city.

Of course we have a bathroom too... and actually, it's kind of high-tech. The floor tiles in the sink area are heated during the winter, and our toilet is the kind that has a heated seat, different flush options (big or small) to conserve water, and a nozzle for washing and drying if you don't want to use toilet paper. And for the bath water in the tub, we can set the temperature to the exact degrees we want with the digital thermostat control.

Fusuma: Sliding walls and doors between rooms. Fusuma are made of thick paper on both sides of a wooden frame. Fusuma slide on tracks, and can also be taken away to make a bigger room.

Tatami: Thick mats made of rice straw and covered with a tightly woven rush grass, and a cloth tape border. Very comfortable to sit or sleep on!

My grandfather grew up in this house, and my father did too. It's been in our family for generations. Someday, when my father dies, the house and land will be passed on to me. This follows the traditional customs in Japan's countryside. These days, not everybody follows these customs, but many still do.

You may see some things here that are different from your house…

We live in a big, old farmhouse.

Shoji: Paper-covered sliding panels. Since the paper is stretched over just one side of the wooden frame, light filters through.

Kotatsu: The heated low table. There is a space heater on the underside of the tabletop, and a quilt between the tabletop and the floor. So when you sit on a cushion on the tatami at the table with the quilt over your legs, you stay nice and toasty warm. In the wintertime, this is my family's favorite place to be: we eat our meals, watch TV, and I even do my homework at the kotatsu!

It's our custom in Japan to take our shoes off before going inside.

Have You Tried Japanese Food?

Traditionally, people in Japan ate rice at every meal, so the word for "meal" and "cooked rice" is the same in Japanese: **gohan**. Nowadays, people eat a huge variety of foods.

When sitting down at table, before eating, you say **"Itadakimasu."** This means, "I humbly receive this food." It is a way to say thanks to the cook.

At the end of the meal when you're finished and your tummy is full, you say **"Gochiso-sama deshita,"** which means "That was a feast," and shows appreciation.

How to Use Chopsticks

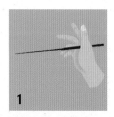

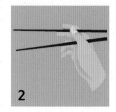

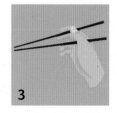

With the proper hand position and a little practice, you can learn to eat with chopsticks! Try these steps:

Step 1: Hold the thick end of one chopstick between the base of your thumb and your hand. Rest the thin end on the tips of your last two fingers, which should be slightly curved. This chopstick will stay still.

Step 2: Then take the other chopstick and hold it between the tips of your first two fingers and tip of your thumb. Curve your fingers.

Step 3: To pick something up, move the top chopstick up and down.

First try practicing on chunky pieces of food, like marshmallows or pieces of popcorn. Then as you become more comfortable, you'll be able to pick up pieces of meat, vegetables, or bites of sticky rice!

A few tips about manners...

Don't spear your food in order to pick it up!
Food must always be pinched between the two chopstick ends.

Don't stick your chopsticks in your rice so that they stand up!
Instead, always lay the chopsticks horizontally on the edge of a dish or on the chopstick rest.

Don't pass food from your chopsticks directly to someone else's!
The proper way is for you to place the food down in between yourself and the other person, on a plate. Then they can pick it up from there with their own chopsticks.

Other foods commonly enjoyed by kids in Japan are noodles (including spaghetti and meatballs), fast food like burgers (sometimes on a rice bun!), pizza (with all kinds of different toppings), and rice with curry. Of course, these foods are eaten with fork, knife, spoon, or fingers—not chopsticks!

Pickles: Eaten at the end of the meal with the last bites of rice.

Bowl of soup: Drunk straight from the bowl!

Hot green tea: delicious!

Side dish, vegetable: Whichever vegetables are in season.

Bowl of steamed rice: It's very sticky, so it's easy to eat with chopsticks!

Main dish, usually fish or meat: Since Japan is an island country, fish and seafood are very common.

A typical Japanese home-cooked dinner has these basic parts.

Okonomiyaki

This is a type of Japanese pancake or pizza. **Okonomi** means "as you like" and **yaki** means "grilled." There's a basic batter and special garnishes, but you get to choose the fillings that you like. You can make it in a frying pan on the stove, but it's most fun on an electric tabletop griddle.

Ingredients

Batter:
• **1 cup flour**
• **1 egg**
• **¾ cup dashi (or water)**
• **1 cup (packed) finely chopped cabbage**

Fillings:
Choose your favorite, or a combination, from these standard choices: *Chicken, Roast Pork or Beef, Shrimp, Squid, Octopus, Corn, Mushrooms, Onion*
(Plan for about ¼ cup for each individual portion, if using two or more ingredients.)

Sauces and Garnishes:
• **Okonomiyaki sauce (or tonkatsu sauce)**
• **Mayonnaise**
• **Katsuo-bushi (dried bonito flakes)**
• **Sakura-ebi (dried shrimps)**
• **Beni-shoga (red ginger)**
• **Ao-nori (green seaweed)**

Steps

1. **In a bowl, mix the batter ingredients with an electric mixer.**

2. **Heat griddle or pan with oil (standard vegetable oil or sesame oil). Fry your fillings until they're close to being cooked.**

3. **Arrange each individual portion of the fillings in a round, and pour about ½ cup of the batter on top. The pancake should be about 10cm (4 inches) in diameter. Flatten with spatula and let cook on medium-high heat about five minutes.**

4. **When the bottom side is firm, flip the pancake and cook another five minutes, until cooked all the way through.**

5. **When done, if making on griddle, turn the heat down to warm and spread the sauces over the entire top of the pancake, and then sprinkle on the garnishes. If making in a frying pan, transfer to a serving plate first, then add the sauce and garnishes.**

6. **Cut into wedges and enjoy!**

Makes 3–4 kid-sized portions

Onigiri

Nigiru means "to grasp or hold in one's hand." Onigiri are rice balls that have a flavorful filling and are often wrapped in seaweed. They are the **perfect picnic food** in Japan. Usually onigiri are shaped as balls or triangles.

Ingredients and Equipment

- A small bowl or cup that is the size you want your rice balls to be
- Sturdy plastic wrap
- A rice scoop or a spoon

- Properly cooked white Japanese rice or "sushi" rice
- Water
- Salt
- Wrappings of your choice. Example: sheets of dried seaweed

- Fillings of your choice. Examples: salted grilled flaky salmon, umeboshi pickled plum, shio kombu (kombu seaweed that's been cooked in a soy-based sauce until tender and salty)

Steps

1. Line the small bowl or cup with a piece of plastic wrap that's big enough to hang over the sides. Press the plastic down into the cup with your fingers.

2. Sprinkle the inside of the cup with a little water. Shake out the excess into the sink.

3. Sprinkle the inside of your wetted, plastic-lined bowl or cup with salt, turning so the sides get sprinkled too. Shake out any excess salt.

4. Fill the cup with rice up to the brim. No need to press down; just fill it loosely.

5. With your finger, poke a hole in the middle of the rice, about halfway down in depth.

6. Put your filling of choice in the hole—about ½ Tablespoon. Lightly press the rice over the filling.

7. Gather up the sides of the plastic wrap. Pulling the whole thing up and out of the bowl or cup, twist and squeeze, pushing out any excess air. Twist the ends of the plastic wrap tightly to form a ball. The squeezing is important, so that the salt sinks into the rice, and to make sure that the rice grains stick together enough so that the ball will not disintegrate when you bite into it.

   For round onigiri you can squeeze and press a bit and you're done. For triangular rice balls, just shape into a triangle.

8. Continue this process to make as many onigiri as you have rice and fillings for. (If you are traveling, you can pack the onigiri just like this, each one in its own plastic wrap.)

9. When ready to eat, take off the plastic and wrap with dried seaweed.

A Day in My Life

My busiest day is Wednesday. When school finishes, I go to ballet class from 3 to 4 PM. Then I have **juku** (cram school) from 5 to 6 PM. Then I go to my calligraphy lesson from 7 to 9 PM. I stop at home in between and eat a quick dinner. Sometimes I'm too tired to do my homework after I get home, which means I have to wake up extra early on Thursday morning to finish it before school.

At school this year, I'm in the 6th grade. This week, it's **my group's turn to serve the school lunch** to our classmates. We have to wear hats to keep our hair back and masks over our mouths to keep germs away. Everyone in the school—students, teachers, and principal—eats the school lunch. We have to eat it all, whether we like it or not! But most of the time it's pretty good. Yesterday we had my favorite: *Oyako-donburi* (a bowl of rice with seasoned chicken and egg on top), side dish of pumpkin with sesame seeds, mixed pickled vegetables, and milk.

At the end of every school day, the last 20 minutes is for **school cleaning**. Everyone pitches in. In our small groups, we all take turns cleaning the classrooms, hallways, stairs, gym, bathrooms (the worst job!), and the outside grounds. The most fun job is polishing the floor: kids race each other across the floor with rags!

On Wednesdays and Fridays after school, I go to **juku**, cram school. Actually, it's fun because I go with my friends, and we like our teacher, Mr. Yamamoto—he's really funny! He gives us worksheets to practice our math, and for writing Japanese **kanji** characters. *(Learn how to write kanji on pages 52–53!)*

It's my father's job to make breakfast for our family. Every day, while my mom gets dressed for work and wakes me up, my dad makes the coffee and toast. Sometimes he makes eggs for us. Sometimes we have cereal. My favorite is **cheese toast and chocolate milk**. Then he leaves for work. He takes the subway to his office. My dad works very hard for a big company, and doesn't come home until late—usually after I'm already asleep in bed. Most weekdays, I only see him at breakfast. That's why he always makes time for me on the weekends. We go to the park, or the **ski-jo** (indoor skiing ramp), or swimming at the pool.

My mom is a professor. She teaches Japanese literature at a university. She walks to work. My mom is a good cook, and we enjoy eating dinner together every night. I tell her all about school and my friends and what happened at ballet or juku. She tells me about the characters in the books she's reading, and about her students.

"My life is busy!"

25

A Day in My Life

My parents are the first to wake up—they wake up early! At about 5:00 AM, they go to the vegetable fields and greenhouse and **pick what's ripe**. Whatever my mom brings back, my grandma will use in cooking our meals for that day. We grow almost all of the food that we eat!

Every morning, my grandma tends to our **butsudan**, the Buddhist family altar. This is where we display pictures of our ancestors. Each morning, my grandmother brings a bowl of rice and some fresh fruit and places them on the shelf as offerings. She lights some incense, rings the bell, and prays to the ancestors of the family.

Once or twice a week, my mother changes the flowers in the **tokonoma**. This is the alcove where a hanging scroll and a flower arrangement are displayed to match the season. If there's a festival, this is where we put the special decorations. *(See pages 30–31 to learn more!)*

After breakfast, my father drives to work. He is a history teacher at the high school.

My grandfather is the one who tends our garden regularly. His favorite thing to do is to take care of his bonsai trees.

26

The first thing I do after I wake up in the morning is to **fold up my bed and put it in the closet**. In my family, we all sleep on the tatami-covered floor. It's very comfortable to sleep on, in between the **futon** mattress and the thick comforter called **kakebuton**. Then I get dressed and go out to the chicken coop. Every two days, I collect eggs from our hens. Sometimes, grandma makes me a fried egg for breakfast—my favorite. Most of the time, we have **rice, miso soup, grilled fish, and vegetables**. My grandparents always say, "Breakfast is the most important meal of the day!"

My sister and I walk to school together with my friend Shota, whose house is on the way. It takes about 30 minutes. We're lucky—some of our classmates live farther away and it takes them an hour to walk to school! My favorite time during the school day is recess and art class. We get recess twice a day, when we get to go outside to the playground.

After school, Shota and I play until dinnertime. We ride our bikes, collect bugs, or if it's raining, play video games at his house.

After dinner, it's bath time. In my house, we have an old wooden **furo**, or Japanese bath. Before dinner, it's my job to put the firewood in the furnace that heats the water. By the time we've finished eating, the water is piping hot, and then we all take turns. Do you know **how to take a bath in Japan**? It's like this: First, in the area outside of the tub, you get yourself squeaky clean with soap and shampoo. You rinse off really well and then you get into the tub. You soak for about 10 minutes, and then when you get out, you put the cover back on to keep the water hot for the next person. My dad loves the o-furo. He says it's the BEST way to relax after a long day!

Sports and Leisure

Kids play sports in school and out of school. Girls often like volleyball and tennis. Boys usually like soccer and baseball best. Swimming is popular among both girls and boys. With their families, some Japanese kids also go to the beach in summer for surfing and scuba diving. In winter, families often go skiing and snowboarding. Traditional martial arts like kendo and judo are popular too.

Annual Sports Day at School

Every autumn, all school children participate in Annual Sports Day. There are **competitions** like running races and gymnastics that test kids' individual skills. And there are **group events** like relays, ball-tossing, and tug-of-war, where you need teamwork to win. It's a day-long, school-wide event, where everyone takes part, and families come out to picnic and cheer on their kids.

Skiing

Across the country, you can find over 500 ski resorts—and many of those also have **hot springs**, for the perfect form of relaxation after a long day of fun on the slopes. In some cities, there are even **indoor ski slopes**, where they keep the perfect ski conditions all year. Japan has hosted the Winter Olympics twice in the past 50 years.

Swimming

Many people, from Japanese businessmen to mothers with their infants to the elderly, go swimming regularly. They swim at health clubs, swim schools, or at the beach in the summertime. Kids learn to swim at school, and some schools even hold long-distance swims, where kids **swim a mile or more** in the open ocean waters!

Baseball

Perhaps the most popular sport of all is baseball. There are **12 pro teams** who play about 140 games each season to compete for the national championship, the Japan Series. Kids play through Little Leagues or school baseball clubs. But the most popular baseball events are the **two national high school baseball tournaments**. One takes place in the spring, and the other in the summer. Teams from all prefectures compete. National news covers the entire event. Millions of fans watch in the stadiums or on TV. There are even special cheers!

Martial Arts

Many traditional martial arts flourish in Japan today, like judo, kendo, karate-do, and aikido. There are important principles that are common to all martial arts. **Aiki** is the practice of matching your opponent (both physically and mentally) in order to defeat him. **Kiai** means fighting spirit, and is important for learning determination and will power. **Kokoro** means you try to improve yourself by cultivating a positive attitude and developing character. **Rei** means courtesy, and is the ceremonial bow that the two opponents do towards each other at the beginning and end of a match; it shows respect.

Sumo

Japan's national sport is sumo. It's ancient, **over 1,000 years old.** Professional tournaments take place six times a year and thousands of people watch in the stadiums and on TV. Two wrestlers face each other inside a ring with only their bare hands. The winner is the one who pushes the other down or outside of the ring. Pro sumo wrestlers **live a very strict life**, including eating a special diet to build muscles and put on as much weight as possible.

Holidays and Celebrations

JANUARY 一月
O-Shogatsu (New Year) is the most important holiday of the year.

FEBRUARY 二月
Setsubun (Bean-Throwing Ceremony) celebrates the coming of spring, when we cast the demons out and invite good fortune in!

MAY 五月
Kodomo-No-Hi (Children's Day) is when families wish for their children to grow up to be brave and strong.

JUNE 六月
During **Tsuyu** (Rainy Season), kids make **teru-teru bozu** dolls to hang in the windows, wishing the sun to return.

SEPTEMBER 九月
During **Undo-Kai** (Athletic Meets) at school, everyone participates in the competitions.

OCTOBER 十月
O-Tsukimi (Moon-Viewing Festival) is when we enjoy the full harvest moon.

In Japan, there is a holiday, festival, or seasonal celebration for every month of the year! It's really fun for us kids. Sometimes Mom makes special foods for the occasion, sometimes we have big family gatherings, sometimes there are fun games and activities we get to do only during that time of year. Check out the 12-month calendar below and the next few pages to see some examples.

MARCH 三月
Hina-Matsuri (Doll Festival or Girls' Day) is the day when families wish for their daughters' health and happiness.

APRIL 四月
Sakura-Matsuri (Cherry Blossom Festival) is when everyone enjoys picnics under the blooming trees!

JULY 七月
Tanabata (Star Festival) celebrates the one day each year when the two star-crossed lovers can meet.

AUGUST 八月
O-Bon (Festival of Souls) is when we welcome back the spirits of our ancestors.

NOVEMBER 十一月
Shichi-Go-San (7-5-3 Day) is to honor girls and boys who are 3, 5, and 7 years old.

DECEMBER 十二月
Omisoka (New Year's Eve) is when we clean and decorate the house to get ready for the new year.

O-Shogatsu (Japanese New Year)

One of the most important traditions is **mochi-tsuki**, the pounding of the special New Year's sticky rice. You put a special type of sticky rice in a big wooden barrel and then pound it with a long heavy mallet. You pound and pound until it's really soft and sticky. Then it's shaped into flat balls called **mochi** rice cakes. The large rice cakes are offered to the New Year gods, and the smaller ones are eaten as part of the special New Year's meal.

Making mochi is a big job that takes lots of preparation, so nowadays, most people simply buy prepared mochi rice cakes in the grocery store. But some people in the countryside still make their own.

O-Shogatsu (New Year) is the most important holiday of the year. Japanese New Year activities start during the last week of December and continue through the first three days of January. During this time, most people travel to their hometowns to spend the holiday with their relatives.

At the end of December, people start preparing for the New Year. It's the time for **the big end-of-year cleaning**, making and sending New Year's cards, and putting up decorations around the house. Traditionally on December 31st, New Year's Eve, families eat a dish called **toshi-koshi soba** (year-welcoming noodles). Around midnight, many families go to the local Buddhist temple to hear the chiming of the bells. The bells are struck **108 times**. This officially marks the transition from old to new.

During the first three days of January, people often go to a Shinto shrine to make New Year wishes, and to receive blessings from the gods for the coming year. When they return to school, students do **kakizome**, the first calligraphy writing of the year.

Make Mochi Rice Flour Cakes

Try this sweet New Year's treat! Actually, many traditional Japanese sweets are made with **mochi**, which is normally white. In the springtime, you might see pink colored mochi for the cherry blossom season. Or mochi that is green is called **kusa mochi**, flavored with a type of herb called yomogi (mugwort). Sometimes mochi has sweet red bean filling inside; this is called **daifuku**. Recently, mochi filled with ice cream has become popular! In Japan, most people buy mochi already prepared. But if you want to try making your own, here's a variation on the recipe using ingredients you can find in the U.S.

Ingredients

- 1 ¾ cup mochiko (sweet rice flour)
- 1 ¼ cup sugar
- ¾ cup coconut milk
- 1 cup water
- About 5 drops red or green food coloring
- Potato starch

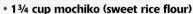

Steps

1. Mix all ingredients in a large bowl with an electric mixer.

2. Pour into microwavable pan and cover with plastic wrap.

3. Microwave on high for 9 minutes.

4. Let cool (about 15 minutes).

5. Dust a flat surface with potato starch. Turn mochi pan over onto surface. Cut into 7.5-cm (3-inch) pieces with a knife (plastic works best because the mochi is very sticky), and lightly dust all sides of each piece of mochi with more potato starch.

6. Pick up with your fingers, and enjoy!

Rat *(Ne)*
2008

Ox *(Ushi)*
2009

Tiger *(Tora)*
2010

Rabbit *(U)*
2011

Dragon *(Tatsu)*
2012

Snake *(Mi)*
2013

Make Nenga-jo Greeting Cards

It is a custom at New Year's time to send **nenga-jo** (New Year's greeting postcards) to friends and family. People do this to say thanks, to give an update on recent activities, to send wishes for a healthy and happy upcoming year, or to share their New Year resolutions.

Usually during the first three days of January, the postman brings a big delivery of all the nenga-jo sent to each family from their friends and relatives from all over the country. Often, these cards are handmade, showing the **eto** (zodiac animal) of the New Year. Do you want to try making your own nenga-jo?

Materials

- **Blank white postcards**
- **Art supplies of your choice (crayons, markers, colored pencils, paint)**
- **Zodiac animal chart for reference: see the rows at top and bottom of this page!**

Steps

1. **Look at the 2 rows of zodiac animals, to find the animal that represents the upcoming year.**

2. **Design the front of your card with the zodiac animal and a New Year greeting.**

3. **Decide who you want to send this card to, turn it over, and write a personal message to them on the back.**

4. **Address the card, put a stamp on it and mail it!**

"I love making cards to send to all of my friends!"

Horse *(Uma)*
2014

Sheep *(Hitsuji)*
2015

Monkey *(Saru)*
2016

Rooster *(Tori)*
2017

Dog *(Inu)*
2018

Boar *(I)*
2020

Inside, a full display might include an arrangement of irises, the seasonal flower; a miniature set of samurai armor, with helmet, sword, and bow/arrow; and folk hero dolls.

Kodomo-no-Hi
(Children's Day)

Outside, people tie carp streamers, called koinobori, in front of the house, one for each child in the family. Sometimes, families include bigger koinobori, too, for mother and father. Carp symbolize courage and strength, and when the wind blows through these streamers, it looks like the carp are swimming.

Children's Day is celebrated on the 5th day of the 5th month. In the past, this holiday was called **Tango-no-Sekku** (Festival of the Iris) or Boy's Day. (Girls had their own festival, **Hina Matsuri**, or the Doll Festival, on the 3rd day of the 3rd month.) Traditionally, this was the time when families with young boys honored them and prayed that they would grow up to be healthy and courageous. After World War II, May 5th became a national holiday, and the name was changed to Children's Day (**Kodomo-no-Hi**).

Nowadays, people honor both boys and girls on this day, and events highlighting children are held all over Japan. People put up special decorations, inside and outside, reflecting Japan's samurai history.

There are also special foods eaten on this day. Chimaki is a sweetened sticky rice treat on a stick that's wrapped in bamboo leaves and steamed. Kashiwa-mochi are rice cakes with sweet bean paste inside and wrapped in oak leaves.

In the past, people also decorated the roofs of their houses with shobu (Japanese iris leaves). It was believed that shobu kept away evil spirits and diseases.

Special bath! At night, when it's time to take a bath, shobu leaves are added to the hot water. This tradition dates back to the time when Japan was a farming society, and the shobu helped to strengthen people to endure the heat and hard work of the upcoming summer months.

Make a Samurai Helmet

Materials

A double sheet of newspaper cut into a square about 53cm x 53cm (21 in. x 21 in.) (if possible, use Japanese newspaper!)

Steps

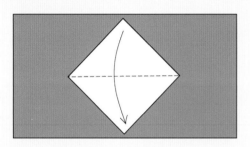

1. Put the square of newspaper flat on the floor or table. Turn it so it looks like a baseball diamond with home base in front of you.

2. Fold second base to home plate.

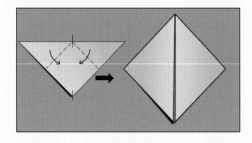

3. Fold first base to home. Fold third base to home.

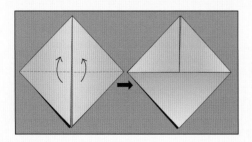

4. Take the right side of the top layer at home base and fold it up to second base. Do the same with the left side of home base.

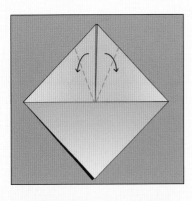

5. Take the right side of the top layer at second base and fold it halfway back to first base. Take the left side halfway to third base. This makes the helmet's horns.

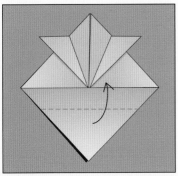

6. Take the top layer at home base and fold it halfway to second base so that the point is about two inches below second base. This holds the two horns in place.

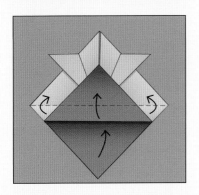

7. Fold the rest of that layer up along the horizontal line between first and third bases. This makes a hat band.

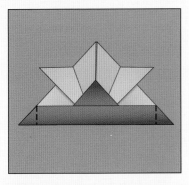

8. Take your remaining home base section and tuck it completely up inside the helmet. Finally, fold the pointed ends of the hat band inside too.

9. Open it up and put it on your head!

A Japanese Folktale

The Legend of Tanabata

Have you ever looked up at the night sky and seen the Milky Way? It is the vast river of stars that spreads across the night sky. Sometimes, on a clear summer night, you can see two special stars in the Milky Way: on one side of it a bright blue star, and on the other side, a dim yellow star. These stars are called Orihime and Hikoboshi in Japanese: the Weaver Princess, and the Cow Herdsman. This is a story about them.

Orihime was a princess who lived in the heavens and whose job it was to weave beautiful robes for the other sky dwellers. She was very talented. She loved weaving and she always sang softly while she worked.

Hikoboshi was a herdsman. He herded his cows all across the heavens. He enjoyed his animals very much and always sang as he walked with them.

One day during his work, he walked close enough in the sky to where Orihime sat working at her loom. Hikoboshi heard something; he stopped and listened. "What is that beautiful melody?" he wondered. "That song is so pretty, it's making me happy just listening to it; I could listen all day…" And he stood listening for a long time.

After a while, he remembered he had work to do. He looked around and noticed that his cows had begun to wander aimlessly. So he quickly gathered them back together and began walking with his herd again. As he walked, he sang his own cowherding melody.

Just then, Orihime finished weaving the robe she was working on. She stopped her loom and stopped singing, and in that silence, she suddenly heard Hikoboshi's song. Now it was Orihime's turn to listen and wonder. "What is that gentle melody I hear?" she said to herself. "That song is so pretty, it's making me happy just listening to it…"

Then, Hikoboshi
walked right in front of
Orihime. The two of them
saw each other, understood
that it was each other's beautiful
songs they had heard, and instantly
fell in love.

Orihime got up from her loom and
Hikoboshi walked away from his cows. They fell
into each other's arms and began singing a whole
new song, a song more beautiful than ever, about their
love for each other.

Orihime and Hikoboshi began walking all through the heavens together,
singing their beautiful love song. They were so happy together and wherever they
went, they brought happiness.

But…no more robes were being woven for the sky dwellers, and the heavenly cows
began to stray wildly.

So the God of the Heavens called them to see him. "Orihime and Hikoboshi, it is clear
that you love each other, and the song that you sing together brings happiness to all
who hear it. But at the same time, your work is being neglected and this cannot
continue.

"I am sorry to have to do this, but I must forbid you to stay
together any longer. You must return to your work! Orihime,
you must stay on the east bank of the Milky Way, and
Hikoboshi, you must stay on the west bank."

Orihime and Hikoboshi knew they could not
disobey the orders of the God of the Heavens. Still,
they protested and pleaded and promised to do
their work if only he would let them stay
together.

Finally, the God of the
Heavens agreed to a
compromise: "If you

promise to work hard, I will allow you to see each other once a year on the seventh
day of the seventh moon. You can be reunited during that time only. We shall call it
Tanabata."

And so it came to pass that Orihime and Hikoboshi were banished to opposite
sides of the Milky Way. On the east bank, Orihime sat at her loom, weaving and
singing her soft weaving song. On the west bank, Hikoboshi herded his cows while
singing his gentle cowherding song. They both worked hard throughout the year,
eagerly awaiting the seventh day of the seventh moon to arrive.

Finally, the day came. Orihime and Hikoboshi were both overjoyed and rushed to
the banks of the Milky Way river of stars. But then it began to rain. It started softly
and gently, but became stronger and stronger, and soon was a raging storm. The
starry river rose in waves so high that it couldn't be crossed.

The storm lasted…and lasted…and Orihime and Hikoboshi soon realized that the
entire seventh day would pass without them being able to reach one another! They
would have to wait another whole year! Their sadness was so deep that it reached all
corners of the heavens.

When the God of the Heavens realized what was happening, he thought…and
thought…and he thought some more. He called the King of the Magpies to ask if the
magpies would make a bridge.

Suddenly, thousands of magpies flew to the banks of the Milky Way, and locked
wings to make a bridge spanning from one bank all the way to the other. Orihime
and Hikoboshi rushed onto the bridge and fell into each other's arms. They were
reunited for the rest of that day, and their song of love filled all the heavens and
brought happiness and joy to all who heard it.

So, when the seventh day of the seventh month comes around every year,
everyone in Japan hopes for clear skies, and they wait for the two lovers, Orihime
and Hikoboshi, to be reunited, and for happiness to rain down from the heavens.

O-Bon (The Festival of Souls)

O-Bon (Festival of Souls) is one of the most important family holidays in Japan. Both serious and festive events take place.

To start the holiday, a **mukae-bi** (welcoming fire) is lit. It is meant to light the way for the ancestors' spirits to return to the world of the living. People visit their ancestors' grave sites, and welcome the spirits back. They offer fruits, vegetables, rice, and flowers at the family altar. Sometimes the local Buddhist priest pays a visit. Then, three days later, an **okuri-bi** (sending-off fire) is lit to guide the ancestors back to the world of the spirits.

On the more festive side of things, at night, people head to the village center or local Buddhist temple, where it's like a big carnival. There's lots of music, dancing, and vendors selling food, toys, and souvenirs. People usually wear **yukata** (lightweight cotton kimono) and join in the big community dance. Learn more on the next page!

For O-Bon, we go back to my father's hometown, where my grandparents live.

My aunts and uncles and cousins join us there. It's a family reunion!

43

Tanko Bushi (The Coal Miner's Dance)

A special community dance, called **Bon-Odori**, is performed at the festival. Everyone participates in Bon-Odori—from grandparents to little kids. They form a circle around a tower stage set up for musicians who play drums, gongs, and flutes. Everyone sings and claps their hands to the steps of the dance as they go round and round the tower. It's great fun! Try it yourself!

One of the most common dances is the **"Tanko Bushi,"** or coal miner's dance. The song is about people working in the mines while thinking of their home in the mountains. The movements of the dance show the miner digging coal, carrying heavy sacks of coal, and pushing carts of coal. Can you make those convincing moves shown on the next page?

The Coal Miner's Song
炭坑節 Tanko Bushi

つ いきが で たでた つ きが で た (アヨイ ヨイ)
Tsu - ki ga de - ta deta tsu - ki ga de - ta (a yo-i yo-i)
The moon is up there. It's just come out. (That's nice!)

みい け たんこうの お うえ に でた
Mi - i - ke Tan - ko no u - e ni de - ta
It's just over Miike Coal Mine.

あんまり え んとつが た かいので (アヨイショ)
A n ma ri e - n totsu ga ta - ka - i no de (a yo-i sho)
Their chimneys rise so high into the sky (So what (happens)?)

さぞやおつきさん け む た か ろ (サノ ヨイヨイ)
sazoya o-tsu-ki-san ke-mu-ta-ka-ro (sano yo-i yo-i)
I'm sure the moon is suffering from the smoke in her eyes. (I'm afraid so!)

How to Do the Bon Dance

1. Dig, dig (right)! Step forward with your right foot and, with your arms, make like you're digging coal. Do this twice.

2. Dig, dig (left)! Do the same on the left side.

3. Heave (right)! Step forward with your right foot and with your arms, throw the coal over your right shoulder into a basket on your back.

4. Heave (left)! Do the same on the left side.

5. Step back (right)! Step back with your left foot while raising your right hand, as if the basket became too heavy.

6. Step back (left)! Step back with your right foot while raising your left hand.

7. Push (right)! Step forward with your right foot and, with both arms, make like you're pushing a cart.

8. Push (left): Do the same with your left foot.

9. pread! Bend your knees and cross your arms in front of your body and then move out to the sides, twice, as if you're spreading the coal on the ground.

10. Done! Clap your hands twice.

45

Say It in Japanese!

Japanese is easy to pronounce. Once you learn the basic sounds, you can easily put them together to form words.

The basic sounds come from the vowels. There are only five vowel sounds in Japanese:

A   Sounds like "ah" (as the a in "**fa**ther").
I   Sounds like "ee" (as the i in "ma**chi**ne").
U   Sounds like "oo" (as in the u in "fl**u**").
E   Sounds like "eh" (as the e in "g**e**t").
O   Sounds like "oh" (as the o in "**o**pen").

Then for a sound beginning with a consonant, just add that sound to the same vowel sound.

These charts show all of the sounds in Japanese. Not very hard, right? You can probably say all of them!

A あ	KA か	SA さ	TA た	NA な	HA は	MA ま	YA や	RA ら	WA わ	N ん
I い	KI き	SHI し	CHI ち	NI に	HI ひ	MI み		RI り		
U う	KU く	SU す	TSU つ	NU ぬ	HU ふ	MU む	YU ゆ	RU る		
E え	KE け	SE せ	TE て	NE ね	HE へ	ME め		RE れ		
O お	KO こ	SO そ	TO と	NO の	HO ほ	MO も	YO よ	RO ろ	WO を	

GA が	ZA ざ	DA だ	PA ぱ	BA ば
GI ぎ	JI じ	DJI ぢ	PI ぴ	BI び
GU ぐ	ZU ず	DZU づ	PU ぷ	BU ぶ
GE げ	ZE ぜ	DE で	PE ぺ	BE べ
GO ご	ZO ぞ	DO ど	PO ぽ	BO ぼ

KYA きゃ	GYA ぎゃ	SHA しゃ	JA じゃ	CHA ちゃ	NYA にゃ	HYA ひゃ	PYA ぴゃ	BYA びゃ	MYA みゃ	RYA りゃ
KYU きゅ	GYU ぎゅ	SHU しゅ	JU じゅ	CHU ちゅ	NYU にゅ	HYU ひゅ	PYU ぴゅ	BYU びゅ	MYU みゅ	RYU りゅ
KYO きょ	GYO ぎょ	SHO しょ	JO じょ	CHO ちょ	NYO にょ	HYO ひょ	PYO ぴょ	BYO びょ	MYO みょ	RYO りょ

46

Now try saying these words!

Oka-a-san (mother)
Oto-o-san (father)
Oji-i-san (grandpa)
Oba-a-san (grandma)
Oni-i-san (older brother)
One-e-san (older sister)
Oto-o-to (younger brother)
Imo-o-to (younger sister)
Aka-chan (baby)

Sakura (cherry blossom)
Tsuki (moon)
Kaeru (frog)

Ichi (one)
Ni (two)
San (three)
Shi (four)
Go (five)
Roku (six)
Shichi (seven)
Hachi (eight)
Kyu-u (nine)
Jyu-u (ten)

Konnichi-wa! (Hello!)

Ogenki desu ka?
(How are you, are you well?)

Hai, genki desu!
(Yes, I'm well!)

Now you can sing the songs on pages 10, 44, and 48!

47

Frogs for Good Luck

In Japan, frogs symbolize good luck. This is a popular Japanese children's song about frogs, usually sung in the spring and early summer, just when the frogs are starting to come out. In Japanese, the sound frogs make is: *"kero kero kwa kwa."* It's fun to sing it as a round, with 3 or 4 people or groups!

The Song of Frogs

蛙の歌 Kaeru No Uta

かえる の　　うた が
Ka - e - ru　no　u - ta ga,
I　can　　hear

き こ え て　　く る よ
Ki - ko - e - te　ku - ru yo.
The　frogs　coming!

く ゎ　く ゎ　　く ゎ　く ゎ
Kwa,　kwa,　　kwa,　kwa
Kwa,　kwa,　kwa,　kwa

けろけろ けろけろ くゎくゎくゎ
Kero, kero, kero, kero, kwa, kwa, kwa.
Kero, kero, kero, kero, kwa, kwa, kwa.

Make an Origami Frog

Here's an easy way to make a jumping frog, by just folding up a square paper. (Hint: the stiffer the paper you use, the farther your frog will jump!)

Materials Needed

A square of paper. About 6.75" x 6.75" (17cm x 17cm) is an easy size to fold, but you can also use smaller sizes. Origami paper works well. Or try cutting an index card into a square, so that your frog will be stiffer. You may want to decorate one side of your paper to make it look "froggy."

Steps

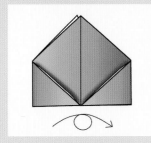

1. Put the paper down flat in front of you. Fold it into a triangle by bringing one corner to meet the opposite corner.

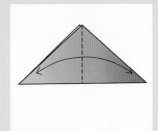

2. Fold in half again to make a triangle half that size. Then unfold this part.

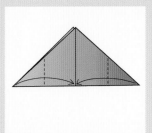

3. Now fold the bottom 2 corners in, to meet at the center of the bottom edge.

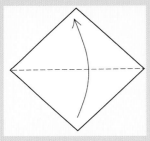

4. Turn the paper over.

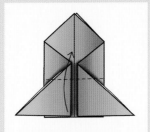

5. Fold the edges to meet in the middle. Let the corners come out from behind. Next, fold up the bottom edge.

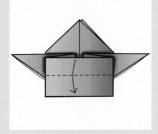

6. Now fold that edge down to the new bottom.

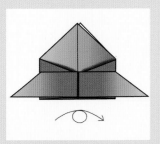

7. Turn over.

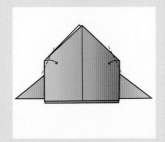

8. Fold the corners up to make the eyes.

9. Now place your frog on the table and press on the back to make it jump!

Do you remember the wintertime **haiku** from page 11? Here's one for the spring or summer!

古池や
Furuike ya
Into an old pond

蛙飛び込む
Kawazu tobikomu
There goes a frog jumping: Splash!

水の音
Mizu no oto
Soft sound of water

—Basho

Japanese Writing

Did you know that there are **three different writing systems** in Japanese? Usually, when you read a book, magazine, or newspaper in Japan, you will see a combination of all of these types of characters:

- **Kanji** is the writing system that came to Japan from China in the 6th century. There are thousands of different characters! And some are very complex, with 12 or more strokes! This means kids in Japan must learn new kanji characters starting in elementary school and continuing through high school. You need to know about 2,500 different kanji characters in order to read a newspaper. **This is the kanji for the word "luck."**

- **Hiragana** is the script that was developed by women in Japan 1,000 years ago. Hiragana characters are simpler than most kanji and are soft and flowing. There are 46 characters to go along with the 46 different sounds in the Japanese language. Kids learn all of the hiragana characters during the first grade of elementary school. **This is the hiragana for the sound "a."**

- **Katakana** is the set of characters that was developed to represent foreign words and names. You can tell katakana characters by their straighter strokes and angular corners. There are 46 characters to match the sounds of spoken Japanese. Kids also learn all of the katakana characters during first grade. **This is the katakana for the sound "a"—see how different it is from hiragana?**

And then . . . kids also learn the 26 letters of the English alphabet, called **Romaji** in Japanese. *That's a lot of writing practice!*

"The first Japanese novel was written by a woman, in hiragana!"

51

Learn to Write Kanji Characters

Try writing in Japanese! There are just a few important rules to remember:

- For strokes going **up and down**: start at the top and move your pen or pencil down.
- For strokes going **side to side**: start at the left and move to the right.
- **The order of strokes is very important**: when first learning a new kanji character, pay attention to the number of strokes and in what order they come.

Go ahead, try writing the kanji for the numbers "1" through "10." Just follow these step-by-step guides!

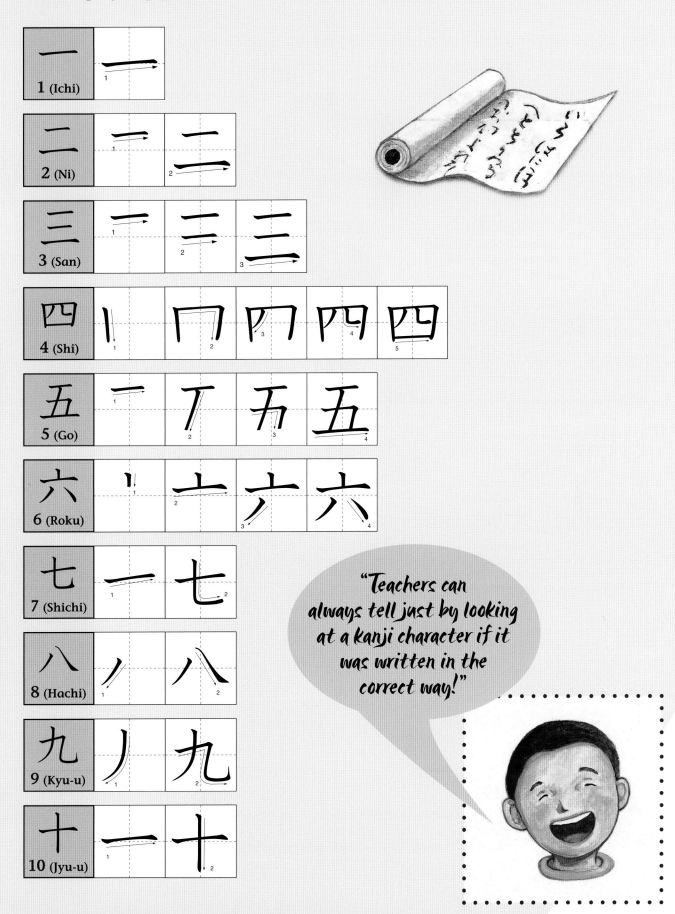

1 (Ichi)

2 (Ni)

3 (San)

4 (Shi)

5 (Go)

6 (Roku)

7 (Shichi)

8 (Hachi)

9 (Kyu-u)

10 (Jyu-u)

"Teachers can always tell just by looking at a kanji character if it was written in the correct way!"

Japanese Culture

Japanese culture is a mix of the old and the new. Many aspects of Japanese culture are popular all around the world.

Video games

Japanese video games have also become popular around the globe. Have you played any?

Budo

Kids who practice martial arts learn discipline and respect while fighting an opponent. In **karate-do**, you use only your hands and feet. In **judo**, you turn your opponent's strength against them. For **kendo**, you wear protective armor and fight with a bamboo sword. **Kyudo** is Japanese archery.

Shodo

To truly master **shodo**, or calligraphy, one must study and practice for years and years. You need to learn the correct posture, handling of the brush, balance of the characters, and rhythm of releasing the ink.

Manga

In Japan, comics are popular among all kinds of people! Elementary school kids often read monthly comic magazines, with many different comic strip stories. For teenage girls, **shojo manga** contain love stories. For teenage boys, **shonen manga** are often action-packed. There are also manga for college students, housewives, businessmen… and educational manga, which make learning about topics like history more fun!

Anime

Animated films produced in Japan are world-famous. Many are based on popular stories from manga.

Ikebana

This is the art of traditional Japanese flower arranging. It is also called **kado**. In this art form, you pay special attention to the type of flowers, stems, container, and how they all work together in your arrangement.

Do 道 "The Way"

Many traditional aspects of Japanese culture end with the kanji character 道 which is pronounced *do* or *michi*. It means "the Way" or "the path." **Budo** means "Way of War" or martial arts. **Shodo** means "Way of the Brush" or calligraphy. **Kado** means "Way of Flowers" or flower arranging. Each of these Ways, or paths, is an art form people practice to cultivate discipline.

Watching a kabuki play is a feast for the eyes! The stage often revolves, and has trap doors and hooks to help the actors "fly." There is a long walkway that extends into the audience, where the actors make dramatic entrances and exits.

Colorful **face makeup** is important to help display personality, mood, and type of character. Usually there is a white base, and then certain colors are used for certain meanings: red shows passion or heroism, black shows evil or fear, green is used for supernatural characters, purple is used for the nobility.

The **costumes** are very bright and showy, including kimono, wigs, headbands, hats, handcloths, and fans. The color, shape, and fabric of the kimono tells which type of kabuki character it is. Sometimes, actors will change costumes in the middle of performing!

The Traditional Art of Kabuki

Drama, dance, music, and visual art—in **kabuki**, Japan's great performance art, you can see all of these at one time! A woman first invented this form of dance-drama in 1603. In the very beginning, only women were the performers, and they danced for male audiences. Soon, kabuki evolved into a popular form of theater where all the roles were played by men. Kabuki remains this way today.

Drama: All roles are acted by men. They play the handsome hero or the evil villain; they also play the young maiden or the wicked old woman. The plays might be about an event in history, or a family drama or romance. Some plays last all day long!

Dance: Actors train for years to master all the dance movements. Some of these are **odori**, the gestures influenced by folk dances, including stamping and leaping into the air; **mai**, circling around while keeping the heels close to the floor; and **furi**, a type of pantomiming, using props such as fans.

Music: Music helps to tell the story. And it provides the dance accompaniment. Some of the musicians sit at the back of the stage; others are off-stage, hidden from view, and provide sound effects. There are singers, flutists, drummers, and players of the traditional stringed instrument called the **shamisen**.

A Japanese Folktale

The Boy Who Drew Cats

Long ago, in a farming village in Japan, a young boy lived with his family. One year, a severe drought destroyed the crops, and many families did not have enough to eat. The boy's parents realized that their son—who was small and weak and spent most of his time drawing—might not survive. So they decided to bring him to a temple, with the hope that he could live there with the monks.

The head priest agreed to let the boy stay. The parents were relieved, and the boy was glad he would have a home and food to eat.

The boy studied, worked, meditated, and ate with the monks. But whenever he had a spare moment, he did what he loved to do most: draw. And what he loved drawing most was cats! He didn't have his own paper; he only had his tools: brush, ink stick, and grinding stone. But whenever and wherever he saw white, wide-open surfaces, he saw cats in his mind's eye and immediately ground up black ink and started drawing with his brush. Pretty soon, he had drawn cats all over the temple—on the floors, on the sliding paper doors, and on blank pages of books.

58

The boy was scolded for drawing all over the walls. But he could not help it. Any time he had a spare moment, the boy drew cats.

Finally, the head priest told him, "It is clear that you are destined to be an artist. You love drawing; it comes right out of you. But we cannot allow you to stay here and continue to draw cats all over the temple property. You will have to go elsewhere. But remember this: Never stay in large spaces. Always keep to small!"

The boy was very sad to leave the temple. He knew he could not go back home because he would be a burden on his parents who did not have enough food to feed the whole family. But where could he go instead?

Then he remembered there was another, much larger temple in the next village. He thought to himself, "Perhaps they are such a large temple, they need someone to be an artist for them. Even if they don't need an artist, I can do other work, like sweeping the floors, or chopping wood. I will go there and offer my services." So the boy took his belongings, making sure to carefully wrap his precious brush, ink stick, and grinding stone, and began walking.

It was a long way to the next village, but the boy walked on, determined. Finally, at dusk, he arrived. He saw the large temple and candlelight flickering

through the windows. He knocked on the front door, but no one answered. "That's strange," he said to himself. "Someone must be there. This is a large, important temple, and there's a light on." The door was not locked, so he went inside.

It was dark. The only light was from the one candle burning. "This is strange," thought the boy. "The monks must still be out working in the fields, since this is such a difficult harvest season. I'll just sit and wait." As he sat and looked around, he noticed it was very dusty and there were cobwebs everywhere. "How strange. It's supposed to be someone's chore to sweep and dust the temple rooms. Perhaps I can do that for them, and they'll allow me to stay." So he found a broom, and began sweeping and cleaning. After a while, the main room was clean, but the boy was tired. And still, no one had returned.

The boy became sleepy and began looking around for a place to lie down. Then, he noticed two paper screens on one side of the room—with bright white paper covering them... and he saw cats in his mind's eye! Immediately, he got out his brush, ink stick, and grinding stone. And he began to draw. He drew cats all over those screens: big cats, small cats, sleeping cats, playing cats. After a while, he stepped back to admire his work. "I have been drawing cats for a long time, but at last they have come out exactly as my mind's eye has been seeing them. They are perfect!"

And, satisfied with his work, the boy now knew it was time to go to sleep. He began to unroll his bedroll... when he remembered the words of the abbot: "Never stay in large spaces. Always keep to small!" So he knew he shouldn't sleep in this huge room. He found a small cabinet with a sliding door—just the perfect size for a small boy like him. He crawled inside and fell asleep.

A few hours later, the boy was awakened in the middle of the night by horrible noises: screeching, growling, and fighting sounds. It

was terribly frightening! The boy didn't dare to peek out from his cabinet. He kept very quiet inside, shaking and trembling with fear. The sounds were awful, and went on for hours. Finally, the ruckus stopped, and the boy fell back asleep.

In the morning, the boy awoke to peaceful silence. But he remembered the horrible sounds from the night before, and knew he had to be brave and face whatever was out there. He gathered all his courage, opened the sliding door, and... jumped at the horrible sight. A huge, monstrous rat-goblin was lying in a pool of blood in the middle of the floor, dead!

After catching his breath, the boy gave thanks that the monster was no longer alive. Then he wondered who had killed it. After all, he was still the only one in the temple. Then he looked at his drawings of the cats on the screens... and noticed that from the mouths and claws of each one, blood was dripping! His beloved cats were the ones who had fought the horrible rat-goblin! They saved his life!

The boy ran all the way back to the first temple, and told the head priest what had happened. The priest was surprised to hear where the boy had been, because everyone else knew that the large temple in the next village had been abandoned after the rat-goblin had appeared there last year. Since then, it lit a candle each night to lure in lonely travelers... and then ate them up! The boy had been very lucky; he had been wise to remember the abbot's warning. Most of all, he had been blessed by his artwork.

And as it turned out, that rat-goblin was also the one responsible for the terrible drought that plagued the farms in the region. Now that it was dead, the rains came back, and the crops grew in abundance again. The boy's cats had not only saved his own life, they also saved the lives of many people in the villages.

In time, the boy grew up to become a great artist, and was known throughout the land. But even after he became famous, every day, he drew at least one cat.

Resources

Further Readings

A Treasury of Japanese Folktales. Bilingual English and Japanese Text. Yuri Yasuda; translation by Yumi Matsunari and Yumi Yamaguchi; illustrations by Yoshinobu Sakakura and Eiichi Mitsui. 978-4-8053-1079-3: Tuttle Publishing Co., 2010.

Japanese Traditions: Rice Cakes, Cherry Blossoms and Matsuri—A Year of Seasonal Japanese Festivities. Broderick, Setsu and Willamarie Moore. 978-4-8053-1089-2: Tuttle Publishing Co., 2010.

Japanese Children's Favorite Stories. Sakade, Florence and Yoshisuke Kurosaki. Book 1: 978-0-8048-3449-0; Book 2: 978-0-8048-3381-3: Tuttle Publishing Co., 2005.

Kamishibai for Kids
www.kamishibai.com/
Comprehensive online source for traditional Japanese storytelling cards.

Japanese Nursery Rhymes: Carp Streamers, Falling Rain and Other Traditional Favorites. Danielle Wright and Helen Acraman. 978-4-8053-1188-2: Tuttle Publishing Co., 2011.

For More Information

Web Japan
http://web-japan.org/
The gateway for all kinds of information about Japan.

Kids Web Japan
http://web-japan.org/Kidsweb/
Best site about Japan just for kids!

The Japan Times
http://www.japantimes.co.jp/
Online version of the most widely read English language newspaper in Japan.

For Materials and Supplies

Asia for Kids
http://www.afk.com/
Multicultural education resource for teaching and learning about Asian languages and cultures. Catalogue (printed and on-line) includes: books, language textbooks, videos, audio cassettes, software, CD-ROMs, dolls, games, posters, crafts, t-shirts, and resource materials for parents and teachers.

Yasutomo
http://www.yasutomo.com/
Good source of art supplies, writing instruments and craft materials.

Asian Food Grocer
http://www.asianfoodgrocer.com/
Excellent one-stop shop for Japanese ingredients, seasonings, snacks, and kitchenware.

For Resources about Japan in the United States

Embassy of Japan in the United States: Consulate General Guide
http://www.us.emb-japan.go.jp/jicc/consulat.htm
Map shows the Japanese Consulate-General offices located throughout the U.S., and links to each of their websites. Find the one closest to you.

National Association of Japan-America Societies (NAJAS)
http://www.us-japan.org/index.html
A private, non-profit, non-partisan organization that offers educational, cultural and business programs about Japan and U.S.-Japan relations to the general public through its member Japan and Japan-America Societies. You can check for a society or center in your region or state.

Index

*To all of the children in both Japan and the U.S. who have
shown me the true meaning of cross-cultural understanding*

—W. M.

For my students

—K. W.

Published by Tuttle Publishing, an imprint of
Periplus Editions (HK) Ltd.

www.tuttlepublishing.com

Text © 2011 Willamarie Moore
Paintings © 2011 Kazumi Wilds

Library of Congress Cataloging-in-Publication Data
Moore, Willamarie.
 All about Japan : stories, songs, crafts, and more / Willamarie Moore ;
illustrated by Kazumi Wilds.
    63 p. : ill. ; 29 cm.
 Includes bibliographical references and index.
 ISBN 978-4-8053-1077-9 (hardcover)
 1. Japan--Social life and customs--Juvenile literature. I. Wilds, Kazumi
Inose ; ill. II. Title.
  DS821.M66 2011
  952--dc22
                        2010040843

ISBN 978-4-8053-1440-1
(Previously published with the ISBN 978-4-8053-1077-9)

Distributed by

North America, Latin America & Europe
Tuttle Publishing
364 Innovation Drive, North Clarendon,
VT 05759-9436 U.S.A.
Tel: 1 (802) 773-8930; Fax: 1 (802) 773-6993
info@tuttlepublishing.com
www.tuttlepublishing.com

Japan
Tuttle Publishing
Yaekari Building, 3rd Floor 5-4-12 Osaki,
Shinagawa-ku Tokyo 141 0032
Tel: (81) 3 5437-0171; Fax: (81) 3 5437-0755
sales@tuttle.co.jp
www.tuttle.co.jp

Asia Pacific
Berkeley Books Pte. Ltd.
3 Kallang Sector, #04-01
Singapore 349278
Tel: (65) 6741-2178; Fax: (65) 6741-2179
inquiries@periplus.com.sg
www.tuttlepublishing.com

First edition
24 23 22 21 20   10 9 8 7 6   2007EP

Printed in Hong Kong

THE TUTTLE STORY
"Books to Span the East and West"

Our core mission at Tuttle Publishing is to create
books which bring people together one page at
a time. Tuttle was founded in 1832 in the small
New England town of Rutland, Vermont (USA).
Our fundamental values remain as strong today
as they were then—to publish best-in-class books
informing the English-speaking world about the
countries and peoples of Asia. The world has
become a smaller place today and Asia's economic,
cultural and political influence has expanded, yet
the need for meaningful dialogue and information
about this diverse region has never been greater.
Since 1948, Tuttle has been a leader in publishing
books on the cultures, arts, cuisines, languages and
literatures of Asia. Our authors and photographers
have won numerous awards and Tuttle has
published thousands of books on subjects ranging
from martial arts to paper crafts. We welcome you
to explore the wealth of information available on
Asia at **www.tuttlepublishing.com**.